The Signs Of Jesus' Return

Will The Millennial Reign Of
Christ Begin By 2003?

Richard L. Madison

Dedication

This book is dedicated to all the Pastors who have invited me to preach the gospel by sharing my testimony and conducting revivals in their churches. By ministering over 300 days a year the first eight years of my ministry, many homes and parsonages have been opened to my family. Thank you, Pastors, for allowing me to warn this generation to flee the wrath to come by preaching this very message without compromise or setting a date about the Signs of Jesus' Return.

Richard L. Madison

Acknowledgements

Special thanks to Religious Products Company in Mableton,GA. for supplying Operation Healing Ministry with audio and video supplies. 800-241-8096

Thanks also to:
Dean & Beverly Garrison of Love Fellowship, Fernando,MS.
Joe and Audrea Perkins; James and Mary Feltman

Contents

RECEIVING END-TIME REVELATION

No one will ever know the day or hour of Christ's Return, the Bible says so. God's Word is forever established. Heaven and earth will pass away, but the Word of God will never pass away. Anyone who has any spiritual understanding of end- time events, would certainly agree that we are in the last days. God is revealing His Word like never before. The Lord told the prophet Daniel, *"Shut up the words, and seal the book, even to the time of the end: Many shall run to and fro, and knowledge shall be increased" (Daniel 12:4).* The seal is being broken on the books of Daniel and Revelation. Many people are running to and fro in the cities and on the highways. The children of God who want understanding are running to and fro from the old testament to the new testament, and vise versa. Knowledge not only has been increased in medicine and science, but also in the Word of God.

I began to receive end-time revelation by the Holy Spirit in 1986, after Jesus raised me up from a twenty-seven day coma caused by an automobile collision. Be sure and get a copy of my testimony in book form titled, **"A Miracle In The Making-Raised From the Dead."**

The Lord began to give me prophetic dreams and visions which have been included in my testimony book, and in the book that you are reading now. I asked the Lord why He had revealed these things to me. The Lord said, *"I have revealed these things to many of my servants, but blessed are your eyes for they shall see and blessed are your ears for they shall hear."* Jesus then went on to say, *"The books are being opened to babes in Christ, and a new generation of believers are being raised up to hear my voice and be my army."*

If we hunger for righteousness and thirst for knowledge and understanding, we shall be filled. The Word of God was inspired by the Holy Spirit in the beginning. It will take the Holy Spirit to reveal the Word of God here in the last days. *"For the prophecy came not in old time by the will of man: but holy men of God spake as they were moved by the Holy Ghost" (II Peter 1:21). "All scripture is given by inspiration of God, and is profitable for doctrine, for reproof, for correction, for instruction in righteousness" (II Timothy 3:16)." The Word of God was conceived in the womb of a virgin by the Holy Ghost" (Matthew 1:20).* Jesus Christ is the Word of God. The Word came down from heaven and took on flesh. *"As many as receive Him, to them have been given the power to become the sons of God" (John 1:12, 14). "For as many are led by the Spirit of God, they are the sons of God" (Romans 8:14).*

These have been born again by the Spirit of God and revelation is given unto them, to guide them into all truth. The Spirit of God will even reveal to them things to come *(John 16:13).* The Spirit of God will always agree with the written Word of God, for He (the Spirit of God) has always revealed the Word of God. The Spirit revealed the Word (Jesus Christ), to John the Baptist. John saw the Spirit come down in the form of a dove and land upon Jesus. John declared Jesus as the Lamb of God which has come to take away the sin of the world. Jesus had the Spirit of God without measure from that day forward *(John 1:32, 35; 3:34)*.

The Apostle Peter received revelation from the Holy Ghost when he declared Jesus as "The Christ, the Son of the Living God." Jesus then told Peter that flesh and blood had not revealed this to him, but the Father which was in heaven. Jesus revealed to Peter, and unto us (the church) that this was the type of boldness and revelation He would build His church upon *(Matthew 16:16-18)*. The Apostle Paul stated, *"That the God of our Lord Jesus Christ, the Father of glory, may give unto you the spirit of wisdom, and revelation in the knowledge of Him" (Ephesians 1:17)*. Paul also said we could receive the same kind of understanding of the mysteries of God as he had received, when we read the Word of God, because revelation comes by the Holy Spirit *(Eph. 3:3-5)*.

The Word of God is a mystery which is hid from the wise and prudent. We must be Born Again to see the kingdom of God. We must be born of water and the spirit to enter into the kingdom of God *(John 3: 3-6)*. We thank God every day for the "logos" or written word. However, it is the spirit that brings life to the Word in our lives and ministry *(II Corinthians 3:6)*. The Spirit of God gives us a "Rhema Word" or a living oracle of what is written. Why? Because the Spirit always reveals the Word. We must take advantage of every opportunity we have to read the Bible, or listen to it on tape and assemble ourselves together at church. This kind of effort allows our mind, spirit and heart to get saturated with the Word.

The Word of God is a sure word of prophecy. It must be our foundation. We must meditate on the scriptures and pray for understanding. The Spirit of God will never say or do anything contrary to the Word of God. The Spirit and the Word must agree together completely. If we do not know the "logos" or written Word, then we may have difficulty in recognizing what kind of spirit is speaking to us.

"Beloved, believe not every spirit, but try the spirits whether they are of God" (I John 4:1). When we hear a voice speaking to us, either verbally, or inwardly, we must determine by the Word of God, if this is Jesus, satan, or our own thoughts. Jesus said, *"My sheep know my voice, they will not follow another" (John 10:3-5).* The Holy Spirit will testify of Jesus and manifest Him to us. The world cannot receive the Spirit of truth, because it seeth Him not *(John 14:17, 21).* End-time prophecy can sometimes only be understood as it unfolds before our eyes and the Holy Ghost sheds light on where the events are in the Bible. Search the scriptures, *"Study to shew thyself approved unto God, a workman that needeth not to be ashamed, rightly dividing the word of truth" (II Timothy 2:15).* You may not agree with everything I have written here, but please search the material thoroughly with the Word of God. You may have to read this book several times to get all this information down. The endtime harvest is here.

May your understanding of escatology (End-time events) be increased by the reading of this book. Jesus is coming soon!

> The Author,
> Richard L. Madison

Chapter One

Jesus Shall Appear In The Clouds

It is now well into the 1990's. The year 2000 is approaching us very quickly. Many Christians have departed from the faith. Many are at ease in Zion and relaxed in this Laodicean Age. When Jesus left this earth in clouds of glory, it was spoken by two angels that this same Jesus would return. Not another Jesus, nor another angel, but Jesus Himself. *"Ye men of Galilee, why stand ye gazing up into heaven? this same Jesus, which is taken up from you into heaven, shall so come in like manner as ye have seen Him go into heaven"* *(Acts l:ll).*

Scripture clearly tells us Jesus shall return just like He left. Very quickly, and in the air. *"For as the lightning commeth out of the east, and shineth even unto the west: so shall also the coming of the Son of man be"* *(Matthew 24:27).* Jesus will not appear in some city at any certain date in which men would foolishly predict. Jesus shall appear in the air. *"For the Lord Himself shall descend from heaven with a shout, with the voice of the archangel, and with the trump of God: and the dead in Christ shall rise first: Then we which are alive and remain shall be caught up together with them in the clouds, to meet the Lord in the air: And so shall we ever be with the Lord"* *(I Thessalonians 4:16, 17).* Not only will Jesus appear in the air, but he will catch his blood bought church up in the air. This event is commonly known as the rapture. Although the word rapture is not in the Bible, we get the word from the words "caught up" in the above scripture. The Greek word for caught up is *harpazo*. It means to carry off, grasp hastily, snatch up or depart. The word *rapture* has been used to describe this event of transporting the saints to meet the Lord in the air.

When we meet the Lord in the air, our bodies shall be changed. *"Behold, I shew you a mystery; we shall not all sleep, but we shall all be changed, In a moment, in the twinkling of an eye, at the last trump: for the trumpet shall sound, and the dead shall be raised incorruptible, and we shall be changed. For this corruptible must put on incorruption, and this mortal must put on immortality" (I Corinthians 15:51-53).* These scriptures reveal that everyone will not die but we shall be changed into new bodies. We will not have flesh and blood for *"flesh and blood cannot inherit the kingdom of God" (I Corinthians 15:50).* I am looking forward to inheriting a new body. After receiving a new body, we will never get sick nor feel pain again. *"And God shall wipe away all tears from their eyes" (Revelation 7:17b). "And there shall be no more death, neither sorrow, nor crying, neither shall there be any more pain: for the former things are passed away" (Revelation 21:4). "He that overcometh shall inherit all things; and I will be his God, and he shall be my son" (Revelation 21:7).*

How Quickly Will Jesus Come

It will only take a split second for the children of God to be changed. In the twinkling of an eye, or, one one hundredth of a second (1/100). This is why we must watch and pray, for

2

we know not the day nor hour, Jesus shall return. We will not have time to get ready when he appears. Luke was speaking to Christians when he said, *"And take heed to yourselves, lest at any time your hearts be overcharged with surfeiting, and drunkenness, and cares for this life, and so that day come upon you unawares" (Luke 21:34).*

Many people who use to go to church and live godly lives have backslid and are unaware of the time in which we live. We know the world shall not recognize the coming of the Lord, but the day of the rapture (which means an event, not a certain time) shall also catch many Christians who are lukewarm unaware. *"Watch ye therefore, and pray always, that ye may be accounted worthy to escape all these things that shall come to pass, and to stand before the Son of Man" (Luke 21:36).* The Apostle Paul told the Thessalonians *"For yourselves know perfectly that the day of the Lord so cometh as a thief in the night. But ye brethren are not in darkness, that that day should overtake you as a thief. Therefore, let us not sleep as do others; but let us watch and be sober. For God hath not appointed us to wrath, but to obtain salvation by our Lord Jesus Christ" (I Thessalonians 5:2, 4, 6, 9).* Paul was not calling Jesus a thief, but rather that Jesus would return when we least expect Him. Nor was Paul declaring that Jesus would return in the night, although it may be nighttime somewhere in the world. Paul was telling us also, not to be asleep spiritually. We know we must sleep in the natural, for our bodies require sleep.

Escaping The Tribulation

Luke told us to pray that we are worthy to escape the tribulation period, for he described tribulation events in Chapter

21. Scripture seems to reveal that the first three and one half years of tribulation, shall be a time of peace for Israel as she offers sacrifices. During this same time, the mark of the beast may be forced upon the world in order to buy and sell in the new world banking system. A time of lawlessness may abound also. This may represent a time of man's wrath upon man. The last three and one half years of tribulation appears to be God's wrath upon man. God shall pour his wrath out on an ungodly world.

The book of Revelation describes events of great earthquakes, fires, hailstone weighing 100 pounds each, wars and rumors of wars, demons unleashed upon the earth, famines and diseases. Anyone who is alive at this time, who has rejected Jesus Christ, and those who have received a mark, name or number in their right hand or forehead shall experience the wrath of God and shall inherit eternal life in a lake of fire. Thank God for the blood of Jesus and the Word of God, for we can escape these things of punishment through Christ Jesus. Jesus said, *"Because thou hast kept the word of my patience, I also will keep thee from the hour of temptation, which shall come upon all the world, to try them that dwell upon the earth. Behold I come quickly: hold that fast which thou has, that no man take thy crown" (Revelation 3:10, 11).*

Who Are The Saints In The Tribulation

Those Christians who are lukewarm, those who believe they will enter the tribulation, and the Christians who are not walking in peace and holiness (which have not overcome the lust of the eye, the pride of life and the habits of the flesh) shall not make the first rapture, but they shall be left behind to be beheaded for the Word of God. *"Blessed and holy is he* that hath part in the first resurrection: on such the second death hath no power, but they shall be priests of God and of Christ, and shall reign with Him a thousand years" (Revelation 20:6). John also saw *"the souls of them that were beheaded for the witness of Jesus, and for the Word of God, and which had not worshipped the beast, neither his image, neither had received his mark upon their foreheads; and they lived and reigned with Christ a thousand years," (Revelation 20:4).* Upon reading these scriptures, we also see that the first catching away, or rapture, will give the saints the authority to be priests or leaders during the millennium reign.

There are two more different kinds of saints who enter the tribulation, and are also raptured in the middle, and at the end of tribulation. The first group of saints entering the tribulation is the 144,000 male Jews. These are redeemed from the earth in the middle of the tribulation *(Revelation 7:1-4; 14:1- 4).* No destruction comes upon the earth until the 144,000 are sealed. These are the first Jews saved after the first rapture. One-third of the Jewish people will receive Jesus as the Messiah at the end of the tribulation *(Zechariah 13:8, 9).* The 144,000 are redeemed before the first trumpet of judgement is sounded.

The second group of saints who are redeemed at the end of the tribulation are the two witnesses *(Daniel 7:25; 12:7; Revelation 11:3, 11, 12).* Jesus will bring thousands of saints back with Him at the end of tribulation, *"Behold, the Lord cometh with ten thousands of his saints" (Jude V. 14). "And the Lord my God shall come, and all the saints with thee," (Zechariah 14:50).* John also saw a number that could not be counted, who were redeemed from the tribulation, *"These are they which came out of great tribulation, and have washed their robes, and made them white in the blood of the Lamb," (Revelation 7:14b). "After this I beheld, and, lo, a*

5

great multitude, which no man could number, of all nations, and kindreds, and people, and tongues, stood before the throne, and before the Lamb, clothed with white robes," (Revelation 7:9). John again saw a harvest taking place during the tribulation, *"Thrust in thy sickle, and reap: for the time is come for thee to reap; for the harvest of the earth is ripe. And he that sat on the cloud thrust in his sickle on the earth; and the earth was reaped," (Revelation 14:15, 16).* Then John saw the ungodly receiving the wrath of God and the battle of Armageddon taking place.

"And another angel came out of the temple which is in heaven, he also having a sharp sickle. And the angel thrust in his sickle into the earth, and gathered the vine of the earth, and cast it into the great wine press of the wrath of God. And the wine press was trodden without the city, and blood came out of the wine press, even to the horse bridles," (Revelation 14:17-19). Jesus was speaking to the church of Thyatira (which also represents a certain church in the world today) when he said he knew their works, love, service, and faith. However, he had some things against these church people. Jesus said, *"Behold, I will cast her into a bed, and them that commit adultery with her into great tribulation, except they repent of their deeds," (Revelation 2:18-22).* We must seek God, repent daily, and present our bodies as a living sacrifice.

We are striving to become perfect. The Apostle James said, *"If any man offend not in word, the same is a perfect man," (James 3:2).* The tongue can bless others or curse others. Christians need to bridle their tongue if they have nothing good to say. Jesus is coming after a holy church, without spot, wrinkle, or blemish *(Ephesians 5:26).* Jesus said, *"He that overcometh; the same shall be clothed in white raiment and I will not blot his name out of the book of life,"*

(Revelations 3:5). If we do not overcome the things of this world, and sin, then we will either die in our sin and miss out on heaven, or we will enter the tribulation period to face death for the Name of Jesus. We can overcome the world though, if we walk with Jesus. He has already overcome the world. Jesus has given us the faith and power. We have the blood, and the anointing, and the Name of Jesus. Greater is He that is in us, than He that is in the world. If we resist the devil, he must flee from us.

"And the Spirit and the bride say, **Come.** *And let him that heareth say,* **Come.** *And let him that is a thirst* **come.** *And whosoever will, let him take the water of life freely,"* *(Revelation 22:17).* More information on the tribulation saints in chapter six.

The Eight Raptures In The Bible

1. The first rapture in the Bible is found in Genesis chapter 5 with a man named **Enoch**. *"And Enoch walked with God: and he was not; for God took him" (Genesis 5:24).*

2. *"And it came to pass, as they still went on, and talked, that, behold, there appeared a chariot of fire, and horses of fire, and parted them both asunder; and* **Elijah** *went up by a whirlwind into heaven" (II Kings 2:11).*

3. This 3rd rapture consists of **Jesus Christ** and the **saints of old** which were raised up with Christ after His resurrection. *Matthew 27:52-54* reveals the graves opening and the saints appearing to many in Jerusalem. In *John 20:17* Jesus would not allow Mary to touch Him because He had not ascended to the Father. However in *John 20:27* Jesus allowed Thomas to put his finger into the nail prints and his hand into His side. Jesus ascended to the Father for a short time to carry the saints of old home and to present Himself with His own blood in the heavenlies in the true tabernacle *(Hebrews 8:1,2;9:11,12,21,22,23)*. This ascension of Jesus was before His forty day ministry.

4. The next rapture was **Jesus Christ** ascending up to heaven after His resurrection and forty day ministry. *Acts 1:3* says Jesus revealed Himself for forty days teaching about the Kingdom of God. *"And when He had spoken these things, while they beheld, He was taken up; and a cloud received Him out of their sight" (Acts 1:9).*

5. The fifth rapture is the **church of believers** who are walking with Jesus as Enoch and Elijah. These are those who are full of the Holy Ghost and fire *(Luke 21:36; 1 Cor. 15:51,52; Eph. 5:27; 1 Thess. 4:16,17).*

6. The **144,000** virgin male Jews and the **saints** who have **already** been **martyred** for the Name of Jesus during the first half of the tribulation period are in the sixth rapture *(Revelation 7:4;14:1-5,15,16).*

7. The **two witnesses**, **1/3 Jewish people** who accept Jesus, and **saints** who are martyred during the second half of the tribulation period (the great tribulation) are raptured at the end of Jacob's Trouble *(Rev. 11:12; Zech. 13:8,9; Rev. 7:14;20:4).* Those who are not involved in the first seven raptures will not live again until the end of the 1000 yr. millennium reign of Christ. *"But the rest of the dead lived not again until the thousand years were finished" (Rev. 20:5).*

8. The final rapture are those who are raised at the end of the millennium reign of Christ *(Rev. 20:5).* This is The Great White Throne Judgement's appearance to judge every man according to his works. Whoever is not found in the Book of Life is cast into the Lake of Fire *(Rev. 20:11-15).* Blessed and Holy is he that hath part in the first resurrection!

Chapter Two

Prophetic Signs Of Jesus' Return

#1 Scoffers

*K*nowing this first, that there shall come in the last days scoffers, walking after their own lust, and saying, where is the promise of his coming? for since the fathers fell asleep, all things continue as they were from the beginning of the creation" (II Peter 3:3, 4). Many people today laugh and scorn when a Christian mentions the coming of the Lord. The heathen laughed at Noah building an ark, until the rain began to fall. It was no laughing matter then. *"For as in the days that were before the flood they were eating and drinking, marrying and giving in marriage, until Noah entered in the ark, and knew not until the flood came and took them all away; so shall also the coming of the Son of Man be" (Matthew 24:38, 39).* Many shall be swept away with the floods of adversity in these last days. Don't let the scoffers stop you from witnessing. Jesus really is coming and we are the generation that shall behold Him.

2 Disasters

"And ye shall hear of wars and rumors of wars; see that ye be not troubled: for all these things must come to

pass, but the end is not yet. For nation shall rise against nation, and kingdom against kingdom: and there shall be famines, and pestilences, and earthquakes, in divers places" *(Matthew 24:6, 7).* Because of technology's advancement in today's world, we have the opportunity to hear and see these types of conditions. With the help of radio, television, satellites, and transportation, we have a first hand look at these events in various places at the same time. The United Nations Assembly are not able to prevent these wars. Even now they are having an expensive time trying to stop the civil wars that are taking place around the globe. We have seen such an increase in earthquakes and diseases, fires, and floods.

One side of the earth seems to be burning up while the other side is under water. Tuberculosis, AIDS, pneumonia, venereal diseases and new strains of hepatitis and strep throat are spreading rapidly. The medical field has very little answers. With the economy sluggish world wide, governments are not able to fund extra research to find the cures. Earthquakes are occurring more often in the United States, even in places that have never registered quakes. No place is exempt in these last days. We watched rescue personnel at work in California, Japan, Mexico, Cairo, South America and what used to be the Soviet Union. The floods and fires of 1993 will take their toil upon the food supply, not to mention the droughts that were before these disasters.

John the revelator saw four major earthquakes during the tribulation period. The first one occurred at the opening of the sixth seal when the wrath of God begins *(Revelation 6:12).* The second major quake is between the seventh seal and the first trumpet during the first half of the tribulation *(Revelation 8:5).* The third quake is during the sound of the seventh trumpet in the middle of Daniel's 70th week

(Revelation ll:l9). The fourth great earthquake is when the seventh vial is poured out which is at the end of Daniel's 70th week *(Revelation ll:l3; l6:l7-2l; Zechariah l4:4-8).* Jesus referred to the day that we live in as, *"the beginning of sorrows" (Matthew 24:8).* What will the evening news reveal next?

3 False Prophets

"For there shall arise false Christs, and false prophets, and shall shew great signs and wonders; inasmuch that, if it were possible, they shall deceive the very elect" (Matthew 24:24). The New Age philosophy is sweeping America. Their ideas of using crystals and meditation and becoming channels to the spirit world are influencing hundreds of thousands. It is believed that one billion Moslems exist now. India, China and other Eastern nations promote idolatry, and America has become a haven for spiritualists. Thousands gather at auditoriums to hear demon possessed people prophesy to them smooth things. These people pay hundreds and even thousands of dollars for tickets to these meetings.

The religions of the world often teach their converts that torture and pain are the way to God. They walk on coals of fire, glass, and nails. Jesus said He was the only way to God the Father. He is the door and any other way reveals them as a thief and robber. *"Jesus saith unto him, I am the Way, the Truth, and the Life: no man cometh unto the Father, but by me" (John l4:6).* *"Verily, verily, I say unto you, He that entereth not by the door into the sheepfold, but climbeth up some other way, the same is a thief and a robber. I am the door: by me if any man enter in, he shall be saved" (John l0:l, 9).*

Witchcraft, satanism, and goddess worship are being promoted in America in such places as public schools, the military and even churches. The airwaves are full of psychic 900 numbers. The newspapers are full of ads purchased by fortune tellers who claim to get their readings from Jesus. Those who do not know the Word of God fall for these false prophets. Many influential people are on television saying, it does not matter what God you pray to, we all are going to the same heaven. This is a lie straight from hell itself.

"There shall not be found among you anyone that maketh his son or his daughter to pass through the fire, or that useth divination, or an observer of times, or an enchanter, or a witch, or a charmer, or a consulter with familiar spirits, or a wizard, or a necromancer. For all that do these things are an abomination unto the Lord" (Deuteronomy 18:10-12). Scripture also tells us in *(Revelation 13:13-15)* that the antichrist will work miracles and even cause fire to come down in the sight of men and cause life to enter a statue which is the image of the beast.

We the believers in Jesus Christ, who are filled with the Holy Ghost, have miracles and signs to follow us today, but we give Jesus the credit and glory for these events. These events are made possible in the body of Christ because the Holy Spirit is still here in the earth. The manifestation of the Holy Ghost is given to every man to profit withal *(I Corinthians 12:7).* Healing is the children's bread. All things are possible to them that believe *(Mark 9:23).* *"He that believeth and is baptized shall be saved; but he that believeth not shall be damned. And these signs shall follow them that believe; In my name shall they cast out devils; they shall speak with new tongues; They shall take up serpents; and if they drink any deadly thing, it shall not hurt them; they shall lay hands on* the sick, and they shall recover" (Mark 16:16-18). These scriptures here speaking about taking up serpents and drinking any deadly thing does not refer to any kind of side show, but rather, the Greek translates to putting away, destroying, or to kill. Our faith should not be used to tempt the Lord, but rather we use our faith to pray for the body of Christ. We do not have to fear if we are bitten by a serpent or drink poison accidentally. Paul was accidentally bitten by a serpent, but he did not worry he would die, for God had given him a commission that he would fulfill *(Acts 28:3-5)*.

When people use the gifts of the Spirit, or proclaim healings and miracles take place in certain lines for certain amounts of money, they are false prophets and are in error. The gospel is free of charge. It is freely received and freely given.

4 Hatred and Ungodliness

"And then shall many be offended, and shall betray one another, and shall hate one another. And because iniquity shall abound, the love of many shall wax cold" (Matthew 24:10,12). So many families are at odds toward one another. Some do not even speak to each other anymore. All it would take, would be a simple "forgive me" but, pride goes before a fall. Many people today are walking around stiffnecked and full of bitterness. Prayers are hindered because of unforgiveness. The devil causes arguments, and lies to many. Satan is the accuser of the brethren. He puts thoughts in our minds, and then accuses us of being evil for thinking such a thing. Satan comes to steal, kill, and destroy. *"For we are not ignorant of his devices" (II Corinthians 2:11).*

"For the weapons of our warfare are not carnal, but

13

mighty through God to the pulling down of strongholds. Casting down imaginations, and every high thing that exalteth itself against the knowledge of God, and bringing into captivity every thought to the obedience of Christ" (II Corinthians 10:4,5). We should prefer our brother, and give honor where honor is due. How can we love God in whom we have not seen, and not love our brethren whom we have seen. *"He that loveth his brother abideth in the light, and there is none occasion of stumbling in him. But he that hateth his brother is in darkness" (I John 2:10, 11a).* Our brother is our neighbor, and people we have come in contact with. We are our brothers keeper. *"This know also, that in the last days perilous times shall come. For men shall be lovers of their ownselves, covetous, boasters, proud, blasphemers, disobedient to parents, unthankful, unholy, without natural affection, truce breakers, false accusers, incontinent, fierce, despisers of those that are good, traitors, heady, high-minded, lovers of pleasures more than lovers of God; having a form of godliness but denying the power thereof: from such turn away" (II Timothy 3:1-5).* All these things are evident in people today. These are perilous times in which we live.

The national syndicated talk shows thrive on getting individuals who are homosexual, lesbian, transvestites, and adulterers. When the Bible is mentioned, slurs and frowns are made along with an outburst of anger. People today pack out sports arenas on Sunday after Sunday, and never think of worshipping God. People loose their voice screaming for their teams, but won't even raise their hands or say "Amen" in church. Revival seems to be spreading in third world countries as people seek God, instead of trying to fulfill the desires of the flesh. Nothing is wrong with sporting events or being with the family at the lake, as long as Jesus is not excluded. Jesus is

14

the only thing that can fill the void in our life. Entertainment will always leave us feeling empty. The Joy of the Lord is our strength. Jesus must have priority in everything we do, and everything we say, if we expect to receive fruit for our labor. Jesus said he would give us fruit that would remain.

5 Dead Churches

"Having a form of godliness, but denying the power thereof; from such turn away" (II Timothy 3:5). "Now the Spirit speaketh expressly, that in the latter times some shall depart from the faith, giving heed to seducing spirits, and doctrines of devils; Speaking lies in hypocrisy" (I Timothy 4:1, 2a).

There are thousands of churches in the world that are spiritually cold, dead, and dried up. There is no life in them, because the Holy Spirit is not welcome. The Holy Spirit will never force Himself on anyone or in any place. *"Where the Spirit of the Lord is, there is liberty" (II Corinthians 3:17b).* Even in America, people are not allowed to worship the Lord freely in most churches. Not because the government stops them, but the religious leaders are the problem. A congregation will only be as spiritual as the leaders are. Then again, if the leader or pastor gets too full of the Holy Ghost, the congregation votes them out.

Many pastors are afraid of losing their jobs at the church, so they simply pacify the people. God needs men and women to stand up for what is right. Don't be afraid of men's countenances. I have been asked to stop preaching so hard before. I have had revivals stopped by the pastor, even when souls were being saved, simply because he was afraid for his job. Most of our churches today, would not even receive the

Apostle Paul, or Luke, or even Jesus if they were here preaching the way they did in their day. *"But these speak evil of those things which they know not, but what they know naturally, as brute beast, in those things they corrupt themselves. Woe unto them! for they have gone in the way of Cain, and ran greedily after the error of Balaam for reward, and perished in the gainsaying of Gore. Clouds they are without water, carried about of winds; trees whose fruit withereth, without fruit, twice dead, plucked up by the roots; Raging waves of the sea, foaming out their own shame; wandering stars, to whom is reserved the blackness of darkness forever" (Jude verse 10-13).*

Our natural minds cannot understand spiritual things. God is seeking a people who will worship Him in spirit and in truth. Not with lip service only but with our hearts. Jesus wants to be lifted up in every service. Even when we are not at a church building, we can still have church, because we are the temple of the Holy Ghost. The Holy Spirit is wherever people are praising God. Many people are sincere in their love for God and they worship in truth. However, they do not know how to worship God in spirit, and often mock those that do. We can be forgiven for anything, except, blaspheming the Holy Ghost.

"Wherefore I say unto you, All manner of sin and blasphemy shall be forgiven unto men: but the blasphemy against the Holy Ghost shall not be forgiven unto men" (Matthew 12:31). If a person does not know anything about the Holy Spirit, they should not make a comment against the things being done, or how He is moving upon people. If they speak against Him, they bring judgement upon themselves.

Many people do not believe God still heals, or performs miracles today. However, Jesus Christ is the same to a thousand

16

generations. He is *"the same yesterday, and today, and forever" (Hebrews 13:8)*. God said he did not do things by his might, or by his power, but by his spirit *(Zechariah 4:6)*. The Holy Spirit is still here today. He is the one who operates the gifts. We are anointed by Him. We must be drawn by the Holy Spirit to come to God. We cannot even know who Jesus is, and even call Him Lord, but by the Holy Ghost *(I Corinthians 12:3b)*. Don't grieve the Holy Spirit, learn to flow with Him and your joy shall be full. The Holy Spirit will never embarrass us.

6 Jews Flooding Back to Israel

"The Lord liveth, that brought up the children of Israel out of the land of the north, and from all the lands wither he had driven them: and I will bring them again into their land that I gave unto their fathers" (Jeremiah 16:15).

One of the most remarkable signs that Jesus is coming soon is the regathering of Jewish people back to Israel from all countries. In 1989, when Communism began to fall in the Soviet Union, over 250,000 Soviet Jews were allowed to leave and most of them went back to Israel. God said he would bring his people back from the North. Directly north of Israel is Moscow. With the help of Moslems (believe it or not), and the United States, Operation Solomon in 1984 and Operation Sheba in 1985 helped transport the Sudan and Ethiopian Jews back to Israel. Operation Moses in 1990 and 1991 helped over 14,000 back to Israel.

In 1948, Israel became a nation fulfilling the words of Isaiah *"Shall a nation be born at once? for as soon as Zion travailed, she brought forth her children" (Isaiah 66:8c)*. Also *(Matthew 24:32, 33)* mentioned the fig tree shooting forth,

17

causing us to know that Jesus' coming was at the door. God referred to Israel as a fig tree in *(Hosea 9:10 and Joel 1:7)*. Israel recaptured Jerusalem in 1967 making it the capital of Israel for the first time in 2,552 years. This is the last generation of the dispensation of grace. More Jewish people shall return to Israel here in the nineties like never before. Especially when Israel begins to reconstruct their temple on Mt. Moriah.

7 The Desert Blossoms

"The wilderness and the solitary place shall be glad for them; and the desert shall rejoice, and blossom as the rose. It shall blossom abundantly, and rejoice even with joy and singing: the glory of Lebanon shall be given unto it, the excellency of Carmel and Sharon, they shall see the glory of the Lord. And the parched ground shall become a pool, and the thirsty land springs of water" (Isaiah 35:1, 2, 7a).

In the northern part of Israel, much drilling and digging has been done to find water. An artesian well has sprung forth. Israel is irrigating water into the desert, forming oasis, flower gardens, and farming. The mention of Lebanon in Verse 2 represents Cedar trees. Lebanon was known for her Cedar trees. Solomon brought Cedars out of Lebanon to build the first temple *(I Kings 5:5-8)*. Cedars are growing in Israel in the desert. Carmel was a city known for her fruit. Israel has a tremendous fruit crop now. They are exporting this fruit with Carmel stamped on it. Sharon was a city known for her flowers such as roses. Jesus is called the Rose of Sharon *(Song of Solomon 2:1)*. Israel has beautiful flower gardens blooming. All of these events are happening because of the pool of water that has sprung forth. Water is even flowing down the Kidron Valley into the Dead Sea. The Dead Sea is drying up in the middle and becoming two seas. One half is still salty while the other half has fresh water flowing in it. *(Ezekiel Chapter 47)* speaks of the Dead Sea drying up and waters flowing. These events are not suppose to even happen until the Millennium Reign begins. John saw a pure river of life flowing out from the throne like Ezekiel did. John saw the tree of life on both sides of the street and the twelve manner of fruits and the leaves were for the healing of the nations *(Revelation 22:1-4)*. *(Isaiah 35:3-10)* speaks of God coming and saving his people, and the blind, lame, and the tongue of the dumb all being healed at once. Then living waters will flow from the millennium temple.

8 The Birds of Hamongog

God also has the birds in place right now being prepared to fulfill prophecy. *"Thou shalt fall upon the mountains of Israel, thou, and all thy bands, and the people that is with thee: I will give thee unto the ravenous birds of every sort"* *(Ezekiel 39:4)*. I have seen these giant birds in the valley of Hamongog with my own eyes. *(Ezekiel 39:11, 12)* tells us the place where these armies are destroyed by God and Israel, shall be the valley of Hamongog. The Israeli scientists state that these giant birds are only in this particular valley.

9 The Battle of Gog

Ezekiel said it would take seven months to cleanse the land. This reveals some type of radiation. It will require professional personnel to bury these bodies which have been exposed to chemical or nuclear radiation. Libya, Persia, Syria, Turkey, and the providence of Russia shall invade Israel in the near future (perhaps before the end of 1996). Ezekiel 39:9 says, Israel will burn the weapons captured for seven years. It is interesting that the tribulation period will last for seven years. Israel may begin to offer sacrifices on the temple mount under a tabernacle while a temple is being constructed. It is preposed by groups of interest in Israel to divide the temple mount evenly between Israel and the Arabs.

Israel offered sacrifices under a tabernacle as Solomon's temple was under construction. "From the first day of the seventh month began they to offer burnt offerings unto the Lord. But the foundation of the temple of the Lord was not yet laid." (Ezra 3:6). Can you imagine what the Moslems will say or do when sacrifices are offered on that temple mount? A Jihad, (a holy war) will start, thus bringing Moslem armies to invade Israel.

Israel is ready to begin temple construction. With the Ark of the Covenant found, blue prints for the temple complete, and several red heifers to choose from, prophecy is about to be fulfilled. Did you notice in the above scriptures that sacrifices were made twice a day beginning with the feast of trumpets. In Leviticus 23:24 the first day of the seventh month was the memorial of the blowing of trumpets. Will Israel once again institute animal sacrifices on the feast of trumpets while a temple is under construction? Only time will tell.

We, the body of Christ, are the temple of the holy Ghost and we need not a temple in Israel to worship our Heavenly Father. We offer up sacrifices of praise and a shout of joy. We know we are redeemed by Faith through the blood of Christ Jesus. We will inherit eternal life with peace and joy by living a holy life without sin.

Back to the thought of the battle of Gog, Revelation 20:8 reveals that this battle will take place again after satan is let out of his 1000 year imprisonment. Some believe that Ezekiel chapters 38 and 39 and Revelation 20:8 are the same battle. Either way we are still on the brink of eternity. The year 1996 appears to be the 2000th year from the birth of Jesus. 1996 is also the year of debate between Israel and the Arabs over Jerusalem from the 1993 peace agreement with the P.L.O. 1996 is the 3000th birthday of Israel, perhaps also the year of Jubilee which was every fifty years (Leviticus 25:11). It could be the 70th Jubilee. There are elections in 1996 for the United States, Russia and Israel. A leader on the rise in Russia, Vladimir Zirvinoski, has already stated that he will invade Israel if he is elected President of Russia. The hooks in the jaws forseen by Ezekiel 38:4 are being reeled in. After the battle of Gog recorded in Revelation 20:8, satan will then be cast into the lake of fire to be heard of no more. Then a new Heaven and earth shall be created with the holy city, new Jerusalem coming down from God where the saints shall live forever, Revelation 20:7-10;21:1-3.

This war may well take place before the next catching away, or rapture of the saints.

10 The Persian Gulf War

We could be watching another war on television take place in the Middle East. This time Israel will not sit back, like she did during the Persian Gulf War of 1991 when Iraq bombed Tel Aviv. Israel will strike back quickly. Israel has over 100 nuclear warheads. *(Jeremiah 50:9)* spoke of an assembly of nations, with Israel, destroying Iraq with arrows. Israel now has a new missile defense (much like the Patriot Missile) called the "Arrow". God said he would send a destroying wind - and fanners to conquer Iraq's brigandine (army tanks), for

Israel had not been altogether forsaken *(Jeremiah 51:1-5)*. Israel has a well advanced Air Force with helicopters (fanners). During the Persian Gulf War (Operation Desert Storm), the United States Army was placed in Saudi Arabia alongside the Syrian and Turkish army. America flew more soldiers and weapons across the oceans faster than ever before. Could Ezekiel have seen some of this 2,600 years ago?

"Thou shalt ascend and come like a storm, thou shalt be like a cloud to cover the land, thou, and all thy bands, and many people with thee. Sheba, and Dedan, and the merchants of Tarshish, with all the young lions thereof" (Ezekiel 38:9, 13a). The word "ascend" means to take off quickly. The word "storm" became part of the name of the war. "As a cloud," represents by air. "All thy bands" implies the United Nations. "Sheba and Dedan" is the same nation today called Saudi Arabia. "The merchants of Tarshish" is the combination today of Syria and Turkey.

The U.S.A. still has soldiers in Saudi Arabia. Could the next Middle East war have similar circumstances only a different conclusion? One thing is for sure, these are the last days. America came out of England. England's symbol is a lion. America, Australia, Canada, Ireland and Denmark are "young lions". The helicopters destroyed 3000 army tanks and 200,000 Iraqis.

11 The Roman Empire Restored, January 1, 1993

"And I stood upon the sand of the sea, and saw a beast rise up out of the sea, having seven heads and ten horns" (Revelation 13:1). This beast that John saw was the same beast or fourth Kingdom that Daniel saw *(Daniel 7:23-25)* which will give its authority to the antichrist for a space of time.

The seven heads represent the seven empires that have or will try to destroy Israel. Six of these (the Egyptian, Assyrian, Babylonian, Persian, Grecian and the last Roman empire) have tried to destroy Israel, and conquer the world. The seventh head represents the sixth empire. It has now been revived and brought back to life *(Revelation 13:3)*.

This new Roman empire is called the European Community (E.C.). It has many members such as (Belgium, Luxembourg, Netherlands, France, Italy, Germany, Ireland, United Kingdom, Denmark, Greece, Spain, Portugal, with Austria joining in January 1995). John saw the beast (which is a world power entity), rise up out of the sea (which represents either people or nations) having ten horns. The ten horns represent ten nations all coming together. Daniel saw three horns, or nations, removed from this late kingdom *(Daniel 7:24)*. The antichrist will remove three countries from the E.C. when he gains power from the E.C. When the E.C. is changed by the antichrist, it will be the fulfillment of the eighth beast John saw.

"And the beast that was, and is not, even he is the eight, and is of the seven, and goeth into perdition" (Revelation 17:11). The Old Roman Empire was in authority at one time, and was not at the time John wrote these scriptures. John saw, by the Holy Spirit, the Roman Empire revised again. This revised empire (the E.C.), will force the world into a "New World Order". They, the European Community, will rule the world the first three and one half years of the tribulation. They then give their authority and power to the antichrist, and he rules for three and one half years. The world is forced to take a mark, name or number in their right hand or forehead in order to buy, sell, or trade *(Revelation 13:16, 17)*.

On January 1, 1993, the E.C. declared that all nations

who trade with her must have a code mark on their products. This mark is a circle with a dragon in the middle. The E.C. has removed barriers at the borders of these nations to enable traffic among themselves without a passport. Much like traveling from state to state in the U.S.A. The E.C. has proposed a one currency by 1996. The new currency has a picture of a woman riding the back of a beast *(Revelation 17:3)*. The E.C. will force the world into a one world bank system, and a one world religious system. The Vatican (Catholic religion) will work with the E.C. and have world power with the E.C.

The Vatican, with leader Pope John Paul II, symbolically blessed Mikhail Gorbachev in Russia, thus winning over many of the Russian people to Catholicism. The Pope also made history in January 1994 by recognizing Israel as a sovereign nation. The E.C. states that she will be in world power by the end of 1996. This mark that was forced upon businesses and products in 1993, may be forced upon individuals beginning in 1999. The antichrist uses the first three and one half years of Daniel's 70th week to gain world recognition and get control over the nations of E.C. He then removes three nations and the remaining nations give in to him. He will use a name and number system along with the mark to identify all individuals.

The Name of the Beast

I have described the "mark" earlier, now let's discuss the "name". The name may not be revealed until the tribulation period. Many names have surfaced over the years, because those names were put in numerical sequence and came out to 666. This is the number of the name of the beast. This number could be put in a bar code much like the one on products and ran across scanners when purchased. A "name" is mentioned in scripture concerning the antichrist, *"And they had a king over them, which is the angel of the bottomless pit, whose* **name** *in the Hebrew tongue is* **Abaddon,** *but in the Greek tongue hath his name* **Apollyon"** *(Revelation 9:11).* These names mean *devil,* or *destroyer.* Perhaps these two names will be put in latin or translated into a numeral system and placed in the hand or forehead. If one takes this mark, name or number in their right hand or forehead, they will be thrown into the lake of fire *(Revelation 14:9-11).*

Microchips are being implanted into animals now that can identify ownership. Governments of the world are now researching ways to put a chip, or bar code on individuals for banking purposes. Also when children are born, if a chip was planted into the foot or hand, a satellite would be able to locate the child in the event he or she went missing.

The armed forces are exploring this option for enlisted personnel to prevent A.W.O.L. or M.I.A.'s. This seems to be a good idea, however, when the antichrist takes control, this will be mandatory. The world is pushing for a world banking system by means of a "New World Order". Many officials claim that this system will be in operation by the beginning of 1997. It all points to the year 1996 and it being a very prophetic year. *"And he causeth all, both small and great, rich and poor, free and bond, to receive a mark in their right hand, or in their foreheads; And that no man might buy or sell, save he that had the mark, or the name of the beast, or the number of his name" (Revelation 13:16,17).*

A computer system is in Brussels, Belgium which takes up three floors of the administration building, and it is called the Beast. Never before has a group of nations had such advanced technology and influence to control the world of trade and identification. Computers now label people with marks, names and numbers.

12 Signs In The Sun, Moon and Stars

"And Jerusalem shall be trodden down of the Gentiles, until the time of the Gentiles be fulfilled. And there shall be signs in the sun, and in the moon, and in the stars; and upon the earth distress of nations, with perplexity; and the sea and the waves roaring" (Luke 21:24b, 25).

In 1948, Israel became a nation. In 1957, the Treaty of Rome was signed by six nations (Belgium, Holland, France, East Germany, Luxembourg, Netherlands) thus beginning the European Community's march toward world power. In 1967, Jerusalem became the capital of Israel, thus ending some of the Gentile rule. In 1969, the U.S.A. was putting the first rocket on the moon. In the 1970's and 1980's man continued to explore outer space. Probes were launched to receive pictures and data. In the late 1980's the Soviet Union launched "MIR", a small space orbiting vessel. The U.S.A. invented a rocket-plane combination (Discover, Challenger, and Endeavor), to be used over and over again. The Hubble telescope was placed in outer space to send back pictures of deep space. It was repaired in December 1993 as men worked outside the shuttle for hours. It has now sent pictures back from as far away as ten to twenty billion light years away.

A hugh celestial of light has been discovered in the northern part of our galaxy. It seems to be moving our way and devouring the darkness of space in the process. Could this be the third heaven *(II Corinthians 12:2)* with Christ approaching to get his people. John said in Christ was life and the life was the light of men. *"And the light shineth in darkness; and the darkness comprehended it not" (John 1:4, 5).* Habakkuk said God came from Teman *(Habakkuk 3:3),* which also means from the North. Even Satan said he would ascend into heaven and exalt his throne above the stars of God. He would sit upon the mount of the congregation, in the sides of the North *(Isaiah 14:13).* Only time will tell what this powerful telescope and deep space probes will reveal about the sun, moon, and stars. Jesus said, *"Immediately after the tribulation of those days shall the sun be darkened, and the moon shall not give her light, and the stars shall fall from heaven, and the powers of the heavens shall be shaken" (Matthew 24:29).*

The book of Revelation reveals four more times the sun shall be darkened *(Revelation 8:12; 9:2; 16:10),* and *(Revelation 6:12)* which is the same as *(Matthew 24:29).* The Day of the Lord will be a terrible day for the ungodly, as his wrath is poured out. Thank God, Christ will restore all things as his feet touches the Mount of Olives and the 1,000 year Millennium Reign begins.

13 America Passes Law To Allow Sacrifice of Animals

In September 1993, the American government made it official by voting to allow animal sacrifice in one's religion. This event happened just before the P.L.O. and Israeli government signed the peace initiative in Washington D.C. It is believed the Israeli government asked the Clinton Administration to pass this law and then the signatures would be given for peace. Israel needed this law passed to keep the animal rights activists off their back when they begin sacrifices.

America gives Israel a lot of support. Israel does not want any hindrances when they are ready to perform these sacrifices.

The ninety-eight vessels needed for the sacrifices should be completely restored by 1996. The snail that produces the purple dye for the high priest's attire has begun to wash up on the Mediterranean Sea for the first time in 1900 years.

The ark of the covenant has rumored to be found and sealed up in one of the tunnels under the Western Wall. I saw an interview with a priest in Israel who stated that he had seen the ark there with his own eyes.

Excavations are being done to find the Red Heifer used to purify the high priest before going behind the veil in the temple *(Numbers 19:1-9)*. Red heifers are being transported to Israel from various sources. Israel wants a red heifer to be born in Israel to make sure certain prophecies are fulfilled. Seven red heifers were sacrificed from the time God told Moses to do so, until the time the temple was destroyed in 70 A.D. Israel sacrificed on the temple mount in Solomon's day under a tabernacle. This was before Solomon's temple was finished *(Ezra 3:6)*. This means Israel may perform sacrifices again before a temple is complete. All Israel needs is an agreement for access to the temple area. This must be the purpose of Israel dealing with the Arabs for a peace covenant.

Thank God, many Jewish and Gentile people are accepting Jesus Christ as the Messiah.

ARE YOU READY FOR JESUS' RETURN?

Chapter Three

Christ Fulfilling the Feast

*B*ut *of that day and hour knoweth no man, no not the angels of heaven, but my father only" (Matthew 24:36).* No one will ever know the exact day, or hour, when Jesus Christ will return for his blood-bought church. There are two reasons we will never know the day or the hour.

First, there are twenty four time zones in the world. Eleven time zones are in what we called the Soviet Union until 1989. There are four time zones in the United States: Eastern, Central, Mountain, and Pacific. Because of the International Date Line, there are two different days or dates in the world at the same time. For example, if someone in the eastern part of the United States said Jesus would return on the twentieth of the month at 8:00 P.M., this date and time would not be consistent around the world.

The *second* reason no one will know the day or hour is because the Word of God declares so. The Spirit of God will never say anything that is contrary to the Word. Some of the Jewish Messianic Rabbis who have accepted Jesus as the Messiah believe that Christ will return for His church at the Feast of Trumpets. Leviticus 23 tells of the seven feasts of Israel. Jesus fulfilled the first four feasts (Passover, Unleavened Bread, First Fruits and Pentecost). Jesus was the sacrifice at

Passover. Unleavened Bread represented Purity and Truth. Jesus is the Truth. The Feast of Unleavened Bread started the day after Passover. Christ lay in the tomb during this Feast. He was raised from the dead after the third day and *"became the first fruits of them that slept" (1 Corinthians 15:20).*

Jesus ascended up in the clouds after walking the earth forty days *(Acts 1:3)*. The disciples were told to tarry in Jerusalem until they received the Holy Ghost.

The first chapter of Acts speaks of 120 people being in an Upper Room. When the Holy Ghost came in like a mighty rushing wind, they began to speak in other tongues, as the Spirit of God gave them utterance *(Acts 2:1-4)*. Seven days after Jesus left in a cloud *(Acts 1:9)*, the Holy Ghost was poured out. Jesus died at Passover and was raised up three days later. He walked the earth forty days after His resurrection. Jesus ascended into the clouds forty-three days from Passover.

The Feast of Pentecost is fifty days from Passover. So forty-three from fifty leaves seven. Seven days after Jesus ascended back to the Father, the day of Pentecost fully came. Jesus said, *"I will not leave you comfortless: I will come to you" (John 14:18)*. So when the day of Pentecost had fully come, Jesus created His church and came back to live in his peoples' hearts, by the Holy Spirit.

The next feast for Christ to fulfill is the Feast of Trumpets. Many believe Jesus was born at or near this feast. He started his public ministry thirty years later, which fulfilled the law *(Luke 3:23, Numbers 4:47)*. Paul mentioned Christ would return at the sound of the last trump *(1 Corinthians 15:52)*,

"The Lord Himself shall descend from heaven with a shout, with the voice of the archangel, and with the trump of God: and the dead in Christ shall rise first; Then we which

30

are alive and remain shall be caught up together with them in the clouds to meet the Lord in the air: and so shall we ever be with the Lord" (1 Thessalonians 4:16,17).

The Feast of Trumpets is called "One Long Day" by the Jewish people. It consisted of forty-eight hours during the time of Christ. It now lasts for thirty-six hours or three days. If Christ were to come on this feast, no one could know the day nor hour, because of the length of the feast. I do know that Jesus is coming, and this is the generation He shall return in.

"Verily I say unto you, this generation shall not pass, till all these things be fulfilled" (Matthew 24:34). Let's research the word "generation". How many years does it last and when did it begin?

Chapter Four

God Warns His People First

S *urely the Lord God will do nothing but He revealeth His secret unto His servants the prophets" (Amos 3:7).* God has always warned His people ahead of time about tragedy, inheritance and world events. God is very precise and He is consistent in revealing future events. Biblical history is prophecy fulfilled. God gives us revelation on numbers and names in the Bible. He reveals his secret plans for mankind. Events are foretold for the past, present, and future. We will explore both numbers and names in this book to unveil God's plan on soon-to-happen earth-changing events.

God uses numbers. For example, one means unity; three means trinity; five means grace; six is the number of man; seven is perfection; eight is a new beginning; twelve equals governments; forty is testing; forty-one means deliverance; seventy represents leadership; one hundred twenty equals completion. I have skipped through these numbers to show an example. Get a book on numbers at your Christian book store. Let us look at the number "forty", first. God caused the flood to occur forty days and forty nights. The number forty represents a time of testing. It can also represent a wicked generation. *"Surely there shall not one of these men of this evil generation see that good land" (Deuteronomy 1:35).*

"Forty years long I grieved with this generation, and

said, 'It is a people that do err in their heart' " (Psalms 95:10).

"*Ye serpents, ye generation of vipers, how can ye escape the damnation of hell. Verily I say unto you, all these things shall come upon this generation*" (Matthew 23:33,36).

Jerusalem was destroyed forty years after Jesus ascended to heaven. The number 'forty-one' represents deliverance. Noah opened the window of the ark on the forty-first day *(Genesis 8:6)*. God used Noah to preach righteousness to the people, and warn them of their wickedness.

Man's imagination and thoughts were continually evil. God destroyed all flesh and everything that was in the earth *(Genesis 6:17)*, except Noah and his seven family members. Eight people were saved by the ark *(1 Peter 3:20)*. Eight means a new beginning.

God is warning this generation today to flee the wrath to come. He has appointed his wrath to be poured out upon an ungodly people. Salvation is for all who will accept Jesus Christ as their savior. *He is our Ark of Safety*. It is believed that Moses lived as an Egyptian for forty years. He fled from Pharoah after murdering an Egyptian *(Exodus 2:15)*.

Moses was delivered from Egypt in his forty-first year of age. He lived on the back side of the desert for forty years. Moses then brought the children of Israel out of Egypt, and they dwelt in the wilderness forty years *(Deuteronomy 2:7)*. Moses was buried by God at the age of 120 years *(Deuteronomy 34:7)*. His life was complete.

After the flood, man's years of living began to decrease. God said, *"My spirit shall not always strive with man, yet his days shall be an hundred and twenty years"* (Genesis 6:3). No one on Earth now shall live past 120 years. Moses, Elijah and Jesus fasted forty days. Saul, David and Solomon ruled Israel forty years. Jeremiah prophesied forty years to Israel and warned them to turn back to God, or they were going into captivity for seventy years. The later part happened, and Israel was taken to Iraq for seventy years *(Jeremiah 29:10; Daniel 9:2).*

Goliath taunted the children of Israel forty days. However, the forty-first day Israel was delivered as David cut Goliath's head off *(1 Samuel 17:16).* Jonah cried, *"Yet forty days, and Nineveh shall be overthrown" (Jonah 3:4).* But the people of Nineveh were spared and delivered the forty-first day.

Jesus walked the earth forty days after His resurrection *(Acts 1:3).* Israel became a nation in 1948. May 14, 1989 Israel began to celebrate her forty-first birthday. In 1989 Communism began to fall. The Soviet Jews were released and allowed to go back to Israel. From 1919 (the year the Soviet Union became a Marxist government) until 1989 fulfilled another seventy-year period of captivity for the Jewish people.

In 1917 the Jewish state was delivered from the Turks by England after another four-hundred-year captivity. Both History and Biblical History have a way of repeating themselves.

In *(Genesis 15:13-16)* God told Abraham his seed would be in a four-hundred-year bondage, and after the fourth generation they would be delivered. Moses was used by God to do just that. This proves that there is a one-hundred-year generation in the Bible (400 divided by 4 = 100). There is also a forty-year generation which was in the wilderness *(Deuteronomy 1:35, Psalms 95:9,10; Hebrews 3:9, 10).*

In *(Psalms 90:10)*, the Psalmist said the days of our years were seventy and perhaps even eighty years. Many people have thought that God has promised us only eighty years; but He has actually promised us 120 years *(Genesis 6:3).* Before the flood, man lived to be six hundred, seven hundred, eight hundred, even 969 years old *(Genesis 5:27)*.

God always warns His people ahead of time. He used Noah to warn his generation while building an ark for approximately one hundred years. God warned Abraham of his seed's future. God warned Israel in Jeremiah's day. Jesus warned the Pharisees of their destruction *(Matthew 23:36),* which was the second forty year generation.

It was forty years from Jesus' ascension *(Acts 1:9)* until Titus and the Romans destroyed Jerusalem. Jesus told the disciples in *Matthew 24:2* that *"not one stone shall be left upon another,"* referring to the temple on Mount Moriah in Jerusalem.

The third generation of forty years, equaling 120 years, was May 1948 to May 1989. God has warned us through Daniel's prophecy that the last seven years before the millennium reign shall begin when the man of sin confirms a peace treaty between Israel and many Arab nations *(Daniel 9:27)*. There are two more generations to consider. *(Job 42:16,17)* said, *"Job saw his son's sons even four generations"*. Job had lived 140 years after his trial (140 divided by 4 = 35 years). This generation equals 35 years. I believe it's possible that Jesus was speaking about this generation of years when He said, *"This generation shall not pass away till all things be fulfilled" (Matthew 24:36)*.

The last generation equals 51.4 years according to Rev. Jack Van Impe's research. *"So all the generations from Abraham to David are fourteen generations; and from David until the carrying away into Babylon are fourteen generations. And from the carrying away into Babylon unto Christ are fourteen generations" (Matthew 1:17)*.

Rev. Impe has done much research into dividing these

generations. Rev. Impe concludes that from May, 1948 (when Israel became a nation as prophesied in *Ezekiel 37:22*) to September 1999 is 51.4 years. Thus, the last generation would be complete near the end of 1999. Another thought on these three different fourteen generations of *(Matthew 1:17)* is that Matthew started with Abraham and stopped at Christ.

(Luke 3:23-38) gives the generations of Christ starting with Jesus and stopping at Adam. Luke gives a fourth fourteen generation (which is Adam to Abraham).

The Generation of a Man

Some of the Jewish people believe that the generation of a man is thirty-five years using *(Job 42:16,17)*. This does not mean that a man will only live thirty-five years, but that he should have a son by this time. We can see this in scripture also. In *(Genesis chapter 11 verses 12, 14, 16, 18, 20 and 22)*, Shem's descendants had children before or at the age of thirty-five. This is after the flood. Before the flood, all people had children when they were much older.

Genesis chapter five verses *6, 9, 12, 15, 18, 21, 25, 28,* and *32* shows how old the people were when their children were born. Before the flood, man lived to be very old. Methuselah was 969 years old when he died *(Genesis 5:27)*. After the flood, man's length of years began to decrease. God caused man to start producing new generations of offspring at an earlier age.

Jesus said, *"But as the days of Noah were, so shall also the coming of the Son of man be. For as in the days that were before the flood they were eating and drinking, marrying and giving in marriage, until the day that Noah entered into the ark, and knew not until the flood came, and took them all away; so shall also the coming of the Son of man be" (Matthew 24:37-39).* The words "before the flood" revealed the thought of an event perhaps after the flood. Also, people were going about their business not taking heed to the warning Noah was giving them. People are doing just that today.

Scoffers today are saying, "Where is the promise of His Coming?" The Lord's coming is closer now than ever before. God always warns His people first. If we multiply thirty-five years, a generation of man, *(Job 42:16,17),* by fourteen, one of the four generations mentioned in *(Matthew 1:17; Luke 3:23-38),* we get 490 years (35x14=490). The number 490 represents forgiveness and a prophetic cycle.

God marked Cain sevenfold *(Genesis 4:15). "If Cain shall be avenged seven-fold, truly Lameeh seventy and seven fold" (Genesis 4:24),* 70x7=490. *"Then came Peter to Him, and said, 'Lord, how oft shall my brother sin against me, and I forgive him? Till seven times?' Jesus saith unto him, 'I say not unto thee, Until seven times: but, until seventy times seven'" (Matthew 18:21-22).*

Jesus wants us to forgive our brethren 490 times a day (if they could offend us that much). We are to forgive one another continually. Let us see in chapter five why God wants us to forgive 490 times.

The Meaning of Jacob's Trouble

I believe Jesus said for us to forgive 490 times because he knew that the Father's plan was to forgive mankind 490 years. *"Seventy weeks are determined upon thy people and upon thy holy city, to finish the transgression, and to make an end of sins" (Daniel 9:24).* These seventy weeks mentioned are prophetic weeks. These weeks equal seven years each. Our weeks have seven days.

The Jewish prophetic week has seven years. Again we multiply seventy times seven (490 years). Proof that a biblical prophetic week is seven years is found in *(Genesis 29:27).* Jacob had worked for seven years to get a wife, whom he thought would be Rachel. However, upon awakening on his honeymoon, he found Rachel's sister, Leah. Jacob's father-in-law told him to fulfill Rachel's week, and work for another seven years. The next seven years was hard for Jacob. In many ways, Jacob's trouble was fourteen years. But the first seven years were not grievous to him. Jacob worked seven years and married Leah (by trickery from Laban). Then he worked seven years for Rachel. Jeremiah referred to the last seven years before the Millennium Reign as Jacob's Trouble.

"Alas! For that day is great, so that none is like it: it is even the time of Jacob's Trouble; but he shall be saved out of it" (Jeremiah 30:7). Daniel said, *"And at that time shall*

Michael stand up, the great prince which standeth for the children of thy people: and there shall be a time of trouble, such as never was since there was a nation even to that same time; and at that time thy people shall be delivered, every one that shall be found written in the book" (Daniel 12:1). Jesus referred to the last 3 1/2 years of Jacob's Trouble as great the tribulation. *"For then shall be great tribulation, such as was not since the beginning of the world to this time, no, nor ever shall be" (Matthew 24:21).* The tribulation period begins when the antichrist confirms a seven- year peace pact between Israel and many Arab neighbors. *"And he shall confirm the covenant with many for one week" (Daniel 9:27a).*

This is a prophetic week which consists of seven years. Many Bible scholars believe the Bible reveals that the church of true worshippers who have been washed in the blood of Jesus Christ will be caught up, or raptured, just before Daniel's 70th week begins. Daniel's 70th week, also called the tribulation period, or Jacob's Trouble, will be a false seven-year peace treaty, broken after the first 3 1/2 years *(Daniel 9:27)*. When Daniel's 70th week begins, Israel will be given the right to rebuild her temple back on top of Mount Moriah, and allowed to sacrifice animals again.

After 3 1/2 years, the sacrifices are stopped, and the antichrist, or man of sin, will sit in the temple, proclaiming Himself as God for the next 3 1/2 years *(Daniel 8:9-14; II Thessalonians 2:4)*. The antichrist also puts up a statue in the Holy of Holies (this is called the abomination of desolation). He causes the statue to speak. He also causes all people that are alive on Earth to receive a mark, name or number in their right hand or forehead *(Revelation 13:15-17; Daniel 12:7,11; Daniel 9:27; Matthew 24:15)*.

At the end of Daniel's 70th week, the battle of

Armageddon takes place. The nations surround Jerusalem to make war with the Lamb of God. One third of the Jewish people are saved and proclaim Jesus as the Messiah, when He returns to destroy the armies of the world. Jesus also puts His feet on the Mount of Olives at this time, and He brings all the saints with Him. The temple is cleansed and the earth is renewed. Christ sits upon a throne in our sight for one thousand years. Satan is chained up in a pit, and no wars, crimes or diseases are found until the one thousand years are up *(Zechariah 14:2-9; 13:8,9; Daniel 8:14; Isaiah 2:4; 35:5,6; Revelation 19:11-15; 20:1-4).* During the tribulation period, *Ezekiel* 42:20 reveals that the Jewish temple shall be built next to the Moslem's temple (The Dome of the Rock), and a wall shall separate the Holy place from the profane. What will the World think to see two temples on Mt. Moriah? One for the Arabs and one for the Jews. A peace process must take place for this to happen. Jacob's Trouble is soon to occur.

Ashes Of The Red Heifer

The Jewish people discovered the Ark of the Covenant in 1983 under the temple mount. They have not made it public but have admitted it on video. I have seen the statement by the leading Rabbi. In 1988 Israel began speaking openly about rebuilding the temple. God told Moses in Numbers 19:1-9 to use the ashes from the sacrifice of a red heifer to purify the priest. These ashes are a must to perform sacrifices in the temple. Seven red Heifers were sacrificed from Numbers 19 to the destruction of the temple in 70 A.D. Before the destruction, Zealots reportly hid the copper container that kept the ashes. A massive search has been conducted for several years by leading archaeologists to find the ashes of the last red

Heifer. There is a difference of opinions by leading Rabbis concerning the ashes of the Red Heifer. Some believe the last ashes must be mixed with ashes of a new red Heifer. Some say just the burning of a new red Heifer would be sufficient. Israel is purchasing red Heifers from various places around the world. An examination must be made upon the red Heifer to be used. It cannot have unusual hair folicles (more than two hairs coming from the same port). It cannot have been used to farm, or any means of a burden placed upon it.

Now spiritually speaking, we the Body of Christ who are born again by the Spirit of God, realize that we are the temple of the Holy Ghost. We do not need a temple in Jerusalem, we are the temple.

When Jesus was crucified, buried and arose again, He became the perfect sacrifice for all of man kind, Jew or Gentile. Jesus became our high priest and access to God the Father. Jesus entered into the Holy Place, obtaining eternal redemption for us by His own blood. The writer of *Hebrews* asks if the blood of bulls and of goats, and the ashes of a heifer would purify the unclean, how much more shall the blood of Christ, who through the eternal Spirit offered Himself without spot to God to purge our conscience from dead works to serve the Living God. For this cause, He is the mediator of the New Testament *(Hebrews 9:11-15)*.

Chapter Six

Why A Tribulation Period?

The purpose of Daniel's 70th week is to bring Israel back into covenant with God. Also, to purge and sanctify the children of God, who have missed the first catching away, or rapture, because they did not repent of their sin. Jesus said, *"And unto the church of Thyatira write, I know thy works, and charity, and service, and faith, and thy patience, and I gave her space to repent of her fornication; and she repented not. Behold, I will cast her into a bed and them that commit adultery with her into great tribulation, except they repent of their deeds"* (Revelation 2:18a,19,21,22). Notice Jesus was speaking to one of the seven churches. He was not speaking to the unsaved people.

We know the people who have not received Jesus as their savior and who are alive prior to Jacob's Trouble shall go into tribulation. Daniel said, *"And they that understand among the people shall instruct many: yet they shall fall by the sword and by flame, by captivity, and by spoil many days. and some of them of understanding shall fall, to try them, and to purge, and to make white, even to the time of the end"* (Daniel 11:33,35).

"I beheld, and the same horn made war with the saints, and prevailed against them. Until the ancient of days came, and judgement was given to the saints of the most high; and

the time came that the saints possessed the kingdom" *(Daniel 7:21,22)*. Jesus said He would spew out the Laodicean church, because they were lukewarm *(Revelation 3:16)*.

"And one of the elders answered, saying unto me, What are these which are arrayed in white robes? And whence came they? And I said unto him, Sir, thou knowest. And he said to me, these are they which came out of great tribulation, and have washed their robes, and made them white in the blood of the Lamb" (Revelation 7:13,14).

Some Christians are lukewarm, and some have habits in their life that make them unholy. Some plainly blaspheme the Holy Ghost by laughing and taking a stand against the Pentecostal or Full Gospel Churches. Blaspheming Christians are not true worshippers, and are not rapture-ready, so to speak.

The tribulation saints consist of several groups of people. One group is the Jewish people, who live under the law. The second group are Christians who are lukewarm. The third group are Christians who have unholy habits in their lives, and the fourth group are Christians who believe they will go into tribulation. *"He that leadeth into captivity shall go into captivity: he that killeth with the sword must be killed with the sword. Here is the patience and the faith of the saints" (Revelation 13:10)*.

Jesus is returning for a holy people *(Esphesians 5:26, 27)*. Remember God told Daniel "thy holy people" have been given seventy weeks, or Daniel's descendants. Jesus said to watch and pray, that we may escape all these terrible times *(Luke 21:36)*. Others were tortured, not accepting deliverance, that they might obtain a better resurrection *(Hebrews 11:35)*. Some people want to go into the tribulation period because they think it is more honorable. Some say since the disciples were persecuted, all Christians must be tortured, but this is not true. Jesus said, *"Wide is the gate and broad is the way that leadeth to destruction, and many there be which go in thereat" (Matthew 7:13).*

Many Christians are bitter, and we are told that without peace and holiness no man shall see the Lord *(Hebrews 12:14).*

Scripture shows us 144,000 male virgin Jews, and the two witnesses entering the tribulation period. However, a catching away will take place in the middle of the tribulation period for martyred saints and the 144,000 male Jews *(Revelation 7:4; 14:1-5).*

The two witnesses, and the 1/3 Jewish people who accepted Jesus, are redeemed at the end of the tribulation period *(Revelation 11:12; Zechariah 13:8,9).* Those whose name is written in the Lamb's Book of Life, who cried out to Jesus and did not take the mark of the beast will be redeemed also *(Revelation 20:4; 13:7,8; 6:11; 7:14; 14:12, 13).*

Whoever does not accept Jesus Christ as their Savior and whoever takes the mark of the beast will not be raised up from the dead to stand before the Judgement Seat of Christ until the end of the 1000 year Millennium reign. At that time they will be thrown into the Lake of Fire *(Revelation 20:5; 20:11-15; 14:9-11).*

Revelation 14:15,16 reveals a harvest reaped from the Earth. So let's see the order of events once more. Christ appears in the clouds for the blood-bought, on-fire church *(1 Thessalonians 4:16,17; Revelation 3:10).*

A harvest occurs in the middle of tribulation (Christ does not appear in the clouds at this event), and of course, Jesus comes back with thousands of His saints and touches Earth at the end of tribulation *(Zechariah 14:5; Jude v. 14).*

45

A harvest shall take place at the end of tribulation also *(Revelation 7:14)*.

The reason people have scripture for three different raptures may be because there are three separate events. The post-tribulationists use Matthew 24:29,30 to prove Jesus will not return for His people until immediately after the tribulation. Of course Jesus will not touch Earth again until the end of tribulation *(Zechariah 14:4)*. Technically, Jesus does not have to appear in the clouds *(Thessalonians 4:16)* for there to be a rapture prior to Jacob's Trouble. For example, Enoch walked into heaven, and God took him *(Genesis 5:24)* and Christ did not appear in the clouds. Elijah was translated to heaven with the appearance of a chariot of fire and horses of fire *(II Kings 2:11)* and Christ did not appear in the clouds here either.

The 144,000 and two witnesses are caught up and no scripture tells of Jesus appearing in these events. God wants us to die out daily now to this world and sin, or do you want to be tortured and martyred and die out for Jesus later? But remember this; if you die in your sins before the tribulation starts you will go to a lake of fire for eternity.

"Now if any man have not the Spirit of Christ, he is none of his" (Romans 8:9b). Pray now that you may be accounted worthy to escape these things and stand before the Son of Man *(Luke 21:36)*.

Chapter Seven

What Event Begins
The Tribulation Period

The truth of the matter is Jesus is coming soon and those that are ready shall be caught up to meet Him. *"Blessed and holy is he that hath part in the first resurrection" (Revelation 20:6)*. When does Daniel's 70th week begin? Let's go back to the thought of the 490 years. God warns His people first, remember?

The Lord told Daniel seventy weeks would be fulfilled before the end of sins took place. God also warned the people by giving them the very event that started the 490-year countdown. *"Know therefore and understand, that from the going forth of the commandment to restore and to build Jerusalem unto the Messiah the Prince shall be seven weeks, and threescore and two weeks: and after threescore and two weeks shall Messiah be cut off, but not for himself: and the people of the prince that shall come shall destroy the city and the sanctuary" (Daniel 9:25,26)*.

The countdown started when the commandment was given to rebuild and restore Jerusalem. Israel had been in a seventy-year captivity in Babylon according to the Word of the Lord, spoken by Jeremiah the prophet *(Jeremiah 29:10)*. Daniel read Jeremiah's prophecy, and began to seek God for the deliverance. God warned Israel she would be in captivity seventy years, and Daniel realized the seventy years were accomplished *(Daniel 9:2-4).*

The books of Ezra and Nehemiah give the account of God stirring up King Cyrus of Babylon in his first year of reign to make a decree to allow the Jews to go back to Jerusalem *(Ezra 5:13). Nehemiah 2:1* reveals the twentieth year of Artaxerxes. This was around the year 455 B.C. From this date until Jesus rode into Jerusalem on a donkey, and was rejected by His own people, and was crucified, fulfilled 69 weeks, or 483 years. It took seven weeks (49 years) to restore Jerusalem. Another 62 weeks were completed from the restoration to the crucifixion of Jesus. He died not for Himself, but for mankind. The countdown stopped at the burial of Jesus. It will start again when Israel signs a peace treaty for seven years with her Arab neighbors *(Daniel 9:24-27).*

From the year 455 B.C., we add the 483 years or 69 weeks, and come to perhaps the end of 29 A.D. It was between 29 and 30 A.D. that Christ was crucified. *Luke 3:23* lets us know Jesus started his public ministry at age thirty. The law required a priest to be thirty to fifty years old to be in the ministry *(Numbers 4:47).*

It is believed that Jesus' public ministry lasted three and one-half years. If we back up thirty-three and one-half years (the life of Christ) from the year 29 A.D., we might be able to place the birth of Christ between the years three and four B.C. From the time Christ was crucified (between 29 and 30 A.D.) to the year 1989 (the year the Soviet Jews were released), four different prophetic cycles (490 years each) elapsed. (29 A.D. plus 490 years=519 A.D.) (519 A.D. plus 490 years = 1009 A.D.) (The year 1009 A.D. plus 490 years=1499 A.D); the year 1499 A.D. plus 490 years=1989 A.D. Remember Luke 3:23-38 revealed four different fourteen generations. This is why we've added 490 years four times.

490 years is a prophetic cycle; thus, the fourth prophetic cycle from Christ's crucifixion ended in 1989. No wonder at this time Israel began to speak about finding the Ark of the Covenant, the Ashes of the Red Heifer and the rebuilding of their temple. No wonder the world began to change, Communism began to fall, and Jews from all over the world began moving back to Israel. A new world order was put in motion. Some noted authors believe Christ was crucified around 33 A.D. This would put the ending of the fourth prophetic cycle at 1993. This would be interesting since Israel signed a peace agreement with the P.L.O. in 1993. More on this in chapter nine.

1967 And The Six Day War

It is possible that 1989 started the last great move of God. Smith Wigglesworth reportedly said the last great move of God would start at the end of the 1980's. He had great revivals in Europe and seventeen people reportedly raised from the dead. He died in 1947.

Remember Jacob's Trouble originally was fourteen years (he worked 7 years for Leah and 7 years for Rachel). If we add fourteen years to 1989 we come to the year 2003. In 1967, Israel fought and won the Six Day War. Jerusalem became the capital of Israel for the first time in 2552 years.

The Gentiles may have lost control over Jerusalem, but this is only temporary: *"And they shall fall by the edge of the sword, and shall be led away captive into all nations: and Jerusalem shall be trodden down of the Gentiles, until the times of the Gentiles be fulfilled"* (Luke 21:24).

Some people think the rule of the Gentiles will be over when the first catching away (rapture) takes place, but Gentiles will be here after the first and second catching away even to the end. Gentiles will fight against Christ at the end of the great tribulation period.

John the Revelator was told to *"Rise and measure the Temple of God and the altar and them that worship therein. But the court which is without the temple leave out, and measure it not; for it is given unto the Gentiles: and the holy city shall they tread under foot forty and two months" (Revelation 11:1,2).*

Scripture reveals that the Gentiles will have access to half the temple mount (Mount Moriah) for three and one-half years. Eventually, the antichrist will set up his headquarters in Jerusalem, and then later destroy the holy city before Jesus returns back to touch Earth and start the millennium reign. Ezekiel saw a vision of the third temple built in Jerusalem and he also saw a wall put up between the holy place and the profane.

"He measured it by the four side: it had a wall round about, five hundred reeds long, and five hundred broad, to make a separation between the sanctuary and profane place" (Ezekiel 42:20). Could the Dome of the Rock (Mosque of Omar), which is the Moslems' temple on Mount Moriah in Jerusalem, be referred to as the profane place? Probably so, since Abraham did not offer Ishmael as the sacrifice in Genesis chapter twenty-two, but rather Abraham offered Isaac up on the altar. Isaac was the promised son conceived by Sara.

Although Ishmael was Abraham's first born, he was not the promised son to be in the lineage of the Messiah. There was another time the younger son received the blessing or inheritance over the elder brother. God told Rebekah that two nations were in her womb and the elder child would serve the younger *(Genesis 25:23).* God was referring to Esau serving

50

Jacob.

When looking back to the year 1967, not only did Israel recapture Jerusalem and make it the capital, but it happened to be exactly fifty years after coming out of the four-hundred-year captivity of the Turkish government (1917 to 1967=50 years); (1517 to 1917=400 years: Israel signed the Balfour Estate with England in 1917 when General Allenby helped deliver Israel from the Turks). The number fifty represents a time of freedom, joy and jubilee.

"And ye shall hallow the fiftieth year, and proclaim liberty throughout all the land unto all the inhabitants thereof: it shall be a jubilee unto you; and ye shall return every man unto his possession, and ye shall return every man unto his family" (Leviticus 25:10). In the Year of the Jubilee, slaves were released, land was returned and debts were forgiven. In 1967, Jerusalem was returned to Israel after the Six Day War (which occurred near the end of 1967). On the seventh day, Israel was marching through the same land that Joshua and the children of Israel marched through after the fall of the walls of Jericho. Joshua led Israel around the walls six days. On the seventh day, Joshua marched through Jericho, the Gaza strip and the Golan Heights. If we add the generation of a Jewish man (35 years) to 1967, we come to year 2003.

I Had a Vision of the Year 2003

The Lord gave me a vision in 1986. I saw a cloud in my aunt's ceiling with the appearance of the Lord standing in the middle of the cloud. Beside his left shoulder was the number 2003. I was fully awake. I had been studying the Word of God. I studied the vision, as it lasted for about forty-five seconds. I asked Jesus what the vision meant, but he assured me that I would understand in due time. Then in May of 1989, God revealed to me that the vision represented the year 2003. He did not say anything specific about the year 2003, but He did say He was pouring His spirit out worldwide starting in this selfsame month and year (May 1989). Prophecy in the Word of God began to be illuminated before my eyes.

Understanding of past and future events began to coincide and join together like a puzzle. Jesus began to put the thought in my spirit of working while it is day. The harvest is now more than ever.

"I must work the works of Him that sent me, while it is day: the night cometh, when no man can work" (John 9:4). I believe a harvest began to be received worldwide beginning in May 1989. A harvest has always been coming forth ever since Jesus came to this Earth, died and was resurrected, but I see this move of God as the latter rain.

"Be patient therefore, brethren, unto the coming of the Lord. Behold, the husbandman waiteth for the precious fruit of the earth, and hath long patience for it, until he receive the early and latter rain. Be ye also patient; establish your hearts: for the coming of the Lord draweth nigh" (James 5:7,8).

A latter rain harvest of soul winning began in May of 1989. From 1989 to 1996 is seven years. From 1996 to 2003 is seven years. A time of harvest is now. When Jesus mentioned working while it is day, He meant for us to be a witness with the help of the Holy Spirit. As we lift up Jesus, He will draw all men unto Him. From 1989 to 1996 may be the time of Leah, or the first seven years of Jacob's Trouble. From 1996 to 2003, perhaps, will be the tribulation period. Daniel's 70th week may begin sometime in 1996. Only time will tell. Joseph had seven years of harvest and then seven years of famine in

His day.

"Behold there come seven years of great plenty throughout all the land of Egypt: and there shall arise after them seven years of famine; and all the plenty shall be forgotten in the land of Egypt; and the famine shall consume the land; and the plenty shall not be known in the land by reason of that famine following; for it shall be very grievous" *(Genesis 41:29-31).* Egypt represents the world. The harvest of plenty represents the harvest of souls for the kingdom of God. The famine represents Daniel's 70th week. If Israel has a seven-year covenant or seven-year peace treaty confirmed in 1996 between her and her Arab neighbors, then truly we the church shall enter into the millennium reign sometime in the year 2003 A.D. I hope so don't you? Remember this is a possibility, I am not giving a date on the coming of the Lord. I am saying that the millennium reign of Christ *must be very near.*

Chapter Eight

The Sixth Millennium

G od always warns His people first. I am reminded of the words of Jesus concerning the revelation of future events. *"Howbeit when He, the Spirit of Truth, is come, He will guide you into all truth: for He shall not speak of Himself; but whatsoever He shall hear, that shall He speak: and He will show you things to come" (John 16:13).*

God wants to reveal mysteries to His people. Although the Lord will never reveal the day nor hour of His Return, we are able to discern the signs of the times. The millennium reign shall be a time of rest for the people of God. Although we will have jobs to do for Jesus, (who will be literally sitting on the throne in Jerusalem), we will not get tired.

"For He spake in a certain place of the seventh day on this wise and God did rest the seventh day from all His works. Seeing therefore it remaineth that some must enter therein, and they to whom it was first preached entered not in because of unbelief: There remaineth therefore a rest to the people of God" (Hebrews 4:4, 6,9). If we endure to the end and remain faithful to God, we not only receive great rewards and a new body, but we also receive a new name. *"But he that shall endure to the end, the same shall be saved" (Matthew 24:13). "To him that overcometh will I give to eat of the hidden Manna, and will give him a white stone, and in the stone a new name written, which no man knoweth saving he that receiveth it" (Revelation 2:17b).* Even Jesus will have a name

that no man knows, *"And He had a name written, that no man knew, but He himself" (Revelation 19:12b).* We will rule the nations with a rod of iron as kings and priests here on earth *(Revelation 2:26,27; Revelation 5:10).*

A time of rest is promised because we are laboring hard for the kingdom of God. The year 2000 A.D. is fast approaching. It will be six thousand years from the time God made Adam until the year 2000. Many Bible scholars have often believed that the six thousandth year or sixth day would end the dispensation of grace and usher in the millennium reign. I have compared six thousand years with six days just as Peter did. *"But, beloved, be not ignorant of this one thing, that one day is with the Lord as a thousand years, and a thousand years as one day" (II Peter 3:8).*

The Word of God is forever settled and cannot change. In understanding the future, one must look at the past. God created everything in six days. On the seventh day God rested *(Genesis 2:2).*

God made man on the sixth day. *"And God said, Let us make man in our image, after our likeness" (Genesis 1:26).* *"And God saw everything that He had made, and behold, it was very good. And the evening and the morning were the sixth day" (Genesis 1:31).* Peter said one day with the Lord is like a thousand years to mankind. A thousand years to mankind is like one day with the Lord. From Adam to Abraham was two thousand years, or two days. From Abraham to Christ was two thousand years, or two days. From the birth of Christ (between 4 B.C. and 3 B.C.) to the end of 1996 should be right at two thousand years, or two days. This totals six days.

"After two days will He revive us: in the third day He will raise us up, and we shall live in his sight" (Hosea 6:2). Shall Christians be caught up to be changed into the likeness

56

of God at the beginning of the sixth day, or six thousandth year? Only time will tell.

If so, we shall live in the presence of the Lord and rest for one day or a thousand years. At the end of the millennium reign, or third day from the birth of Christ, we will enter the seventh day. At this time, new Jerusalem comes down. *"And I saw a new heaven and a new earth: for the first heaven and the first earth were passed away; and there was no more sea. And I John saw the holy city, New Jerusalem, coming down from God out of heaven, prepared as a bride adorned for her husband. And God shall wipe away all tears from their eyes; and there shall be no more death, neither sorrow, nor crying, neither shall there by any more pain: for the former things are passed away (Revelation 21:1,2,4).*

John 2:1 reveals Jesus at a marriage feast on the third day. Verse six of this same chapter says Jesus called for the six waterpots used to purify the Jews. It is interesting to think of Jesus using 6000 years (not six waterpots) to purify mankind. Jesus turned the water into wine in verse nine. The governor of the feast was amazed that the wine tasted better than the wine that was set out at the beginning. The wine represents the anointing of God. Jesus wants us to know that the anointing will be greater and stronger and more plentiful here at the end of this last dispensation than it has ever been before. Since sin is much more on the rise, the grace of God does much more abound *(Romans 5:20)*.

The Final Sign Before The Sixth Millennium

Many people are looking for a sign to warn them before Jesus comes back or before the world enters a new era. The Pharisees ask for a sign to let them know if Jesus was the

Messiah. They ask for a sign from heaven. *"He answered and said unto them, when it is evening, ye say, it will be fair weather: for the sky is red. And in the morning, it will be foul weather today: for the sky is red and lowering. Oh ye hypocrites, ye can discern the face of the sky; but can ye not discern the signs of the times? A wicked and adulterous generation seekth after a sign; and there shall no sign be given unto it, but the sign of the prophet Jonas. And he left them and departed" (Matt. 16:1-4).*

God is raising up an army of Jonah's to cry aloud and spare not. The word of the Lord came to Jonah a second time *(Jonah 3:1)*. The Spirit of the Lord is speaking to his people through his prophets again. The prophets of the Lord have gone their own way but now are arising to warn Nineveh (the world) that things are going to happen in so many days. A cry began in 1988 throughout America with a book called (88 Reasons Why Jesus Is Coming In 1988). Many people are serving God today because of that warning. The author of that book made a terrible mistake in choosing a certain date (September 13, 1988) in which Jesus would return. We will never know the day nor hour of Christ's return. June 9, 1994 was declared a date in which evil would be removed for a time. Some said catastrophic events would begin. These are the signs of the prophet Jonah. Whether we see anything take place or not, more warnings will be given. A generation of people will hear and repent, just as the days of Ninevah, when 120,000 people came to the Lord. You will hear more frequent alarms in these last days to prepare for the coming of the Lord. God will not repent of His anger this time. Judgement will come upon the world. We are the warning. Arise, cry aloud and spare not!!

Chapter Nine

The Peace Treaty Of 1993

In September of 1993, the P.L.O. (Palestine Liberation Organization) and the Israeli government signed a document to begin a peace process. This would also put in motion for the P.L.O. to govern themselves and Israeli forces to withdraw from the occupied territories. This document is called the "Doctrine of Principles". This could initiate a covenant or peace treaty between Israel and her Arab neighbors in our generation. The Foreign Minister of Israel, Shimon Peres, signed the document on the White House lawn. This document is not the covenant being confirmed by the antichrist, nor does this signing start Daniel's 70th week, but it is the forerunner. Eventually a peace treaty will be confirmed and Shimon Peres may be involved. The name Peres (spelled three ways, Pharez, Perez and Peres), means a broken agreement, or a breach. *"And it came to pass, as he drew back his hand, that behold, his brother came out: and she said, How has thou broken forth? This breach be upon thee: therefore his name was called Pharez" (Genesis 38:29).*

Judah had gone into his daughter-in-law, Tamar, unaware, for she had put a veil on. She conceived and bore twins. The child to break forth first withdrew and Pharez came out first. Thus Pharez received the blessing of the firstborn. The second time the name Pharez is used is found in II Samuel.

"And the anger of the Lord was kindled against Uzzah; and God smote him there for his error; and there he died by the ark of God. And David was displeased, because the Lord had made a breach upon Uzzah: and he called the name of the place Perez-Uzzah to this day" (II Samuel 6:7,8). We can see how Shimon Peres may be involved in the signing of Daniel's 70th week, since his name means a breach. The seven-year peace treaty shall be broken in the middle.

God uses names and numbers to fulfill events, and warn his people. Even the Prime Minister of Israel, Yitzak Rabim, could be a warning that this is the generation the 70th week of Daniel will be fulfilled. It is interesting to note that the antichrist will *"confirm the covenant with many for one week" (Daniel 9:27).* The word *many* is derived from the Hebrew root word *rav* or *rab* and also translates *ravin* or *rabim*. It means *great* or *multitude*. From this root comes the familiar word *rabbi*. The word *many* may represent a certain leader of Israel (Yitzak Rabim?) or perhaps a group of leaders of Israel or even a combination of a leader (leaders) from Israel and neighboring Arab nations.

Scripture does not say that he, or antichrist, will make up a covenant or agreement. Rather, he will strengthen one, perhaps already in existence. Although Israel had a similar agreement with Rome in the first century, it is obvious that that covenant was not the last seven years before the millennium reign. Many Bible scholars believe that the antichrist will be a great political leader representing the globalized Roman Empire. As of January 1, 1993, the European Community, or the old Roman Empire revised, became a reality, pushing forth a "new world order".

The antichrist will honor the "covenant" he "confirms", or strengthens with Israel, for only half of the said seven years.

The word *confirms*, when used as a verb, means to strengthen, or make strong, or acknowledge. Israel and the P.L.O. signed another agreement on May 4, 1994 to allow the Palestinians to begin to start their own statehood. I do not believe this will last. Israel will continue to have clashes with the P.L.O. and will probably annul these agreements. This will cause the Arab World to invade Israel and Israel will destroy these armies, thus fulfilling *Ezekiel 38 and 39*. Perhaps it will be after this invasion that the antichrist is able to confirm the covenant and allow Israel to begin sacrifices on Mount Moriah again.

Who Are The Beast And False Prophet

The European Community (E.C.) will give it's authority to the antichrist *(Rev. 17:12,13)* for a space of time. The antichrist or second beast *(Rev. 13:11)*, will exalt the first beast or European Community *(Rev. 13:12)*. The E.C. will give authority to the Pope of Rome, Italy; the leader of Catholicism. He will declare a one world religion *(Rev. 17:1-9)*. The Vatican has the influence of millions of people, the riches of the world, and it sits upon seven mountains in Rome. The E.C. is the old Roman empire revised again. It is the seventh head that has come back to life *(Rev. 13:2)*. The antichrist will remove three nations from the E.C. *(Daniel 7:20)*, thus causing the E.C. to become the eighth beast from the seventh *(Rev. 17:11)*. The Pope appears to become the false prophet near the end of the first half of the tribulation period. The false prophet will proclaim the antichrist as God before the world. The antichrist will turn on the E.C. and also break the seven year peace agreement. He will set his headquarters in Jerusalem. The E.C. will turn on the Vatican. The last 3 1/2 years of the treaty will be the great tribulation. At the end of the great tribulation, the

Battle of Armageddon takes place. The antichrist and false prophet are thrown in the Lake of Fire. Satan is bound for a thousand years. The millennium reign begins. Alleluia!! See scripture reference in *(Rev. 19:20; 17:13-18); (Matt. 24:15,21); (Dan. 11:31,45); (II Thess. 2:4)*.

Who Are The Two Witnesses

"And I will give power unto my two witnesses, and they shall prophesy 1260 days, clothed in sackcloth. These are the two olive trees and the two candlesticks standing before the God of the earth. These have power to shut heaven, that it rain not in the days of their prophecy: and have power over waters to turn them to blood, and to smite the earth will all plagues, as often as they will" (Rev. 11:3,4,6). The two witnesses carry out judgement on the earth. The exact plagues that Elijah and Moses carried out in their day. Elijah shut up the heavens that it rained not for 3 1/2 years *(I Kings 17:1; 7; James 5:17)*. Moses brought plagues upon Egypt and turned the water into blood *(Exodus 7:3, 17-21)*. People have suggested Enoch and Elijah because these two never saw physical death. *"And as it is appointed unto men once to die, but after this the judgement" (Hebrews 9:27)*. Paul told us that everyone will not die. *"We shall not all sleep, but we all shall be changed" (I Cor. 15:51)*. *"Then we which are alive and remain shall be caught up" (I Thess. 4:17)*. Satan argued with Michael the archangel over the body of Moses *(Jude v. 9)*. More proof that Elijah and Moses are the two candlesticks, olive trees, or anointed ones that stand by the Lord of the whole earth is in *Matt. 17:3*, *"And behold, there appeared unto them Moses and Elias talking with Him."* Jesus was on the mount of transfiguration. Moses and Elijah were transfigured with Him.

Chapter Ten

The Covenant of Jerusalem

On May 19, 1993 a document called the Covenant of Jerusalem was affirmed by seventy leaders of world jewry. Over 1,500 top brass of the Israeli government were on hand for the signing. The number seventy represented leadership in Moses' day. *"And the Lord said unto Moses, Gather unto me seventy men of the elders of Israel, whom thou knowest to be the elders of the people" (Numbers 11:16A).* The New Testament revealed a "council of seventy" called the Sanhedrin who were used to discuss important questions concerning Israel. The Jerusalem Post of June 6, 1992 stated the covenant would consist of seven paragraphs (seven representing the Sabbath, the sabbatical year, the seven metaphorical walls surrounding Jerusalem, and the seven gates of the temple). See document on page 66.

While Israel searches for peace, scripture declares there will be no peace until Jesus sets up his millennium kingdom. *"To wit, the prophets of Israel which prophesy concerning Jerusalem, and which see vision of peace for her, and there is no peace, saith the Lord" (Ezekiel 13:16).*

"For when they shall say, Peace and Safety; then sudden destruction cometh upon them, as travail upon a woman with child; and they shall not escape" (II Thessalonians 5:3).

"Strengthen ye the weak hands and confirm the feeble knees. Say to them that are of a fearful heart Be strong, fear not: behold, your God will come with vengeance, even God with a recompense; He will come and save you. Then the eyes of the blind shall be opened and the ears of the deaf shall be unstopped. Then shall the lame man leap as a hart and the tongue of the dumb sing and a highway shall be there, and a way, and it shall be called the Way of Holiness, the unclean shall not pass over it. No lion shall be there, nor any ravenous beast shall go up thereon, it shall not be found there; but the redeemed shall walk there: and the ransomed of the Lord shall return, and come to Zion with songs and everlasting joy upon their heads; they shall obtain joy and gladness, and sorrow and sighing shall flee away" (Isaiah 35:3-10).

Praise God, there is coming a day when there will be no blind, halt or withered. This shall be during a thousand year millennium reign. The word millennium means one thousand. After the seven year period (Jacob's Trouble) is over, the Earth shall be renewed by Christ. After the Millennium Reign, the New Jerusalem shall come down, the dimensions of which are 1500 miles square! *(Revelation 21:1,2,16).*

Are you ready to meet your maker? Are you born again? Do you really know who Jesus is; or have you just joined a church? Repent and pray for Jesus to reveal Himself to you right now. Seek the Lord and you shall find Him. This is your day of salvation. We are not promised tomorrow. Believe in your heart and confess with your mouth that Jesus Christ is Lord!

*F**ather, I come to You in the name of Your son, Jesus Christ, confessing with my mouth and believing in my heart according to Your Word in **Romans 10:9** that*

Jesus died for my sins and was dead three days. Father, You raised Jesus from the dead and now He intercedes in my behalf. I am a sinner and I have fallen short of the glory of God, but I am now being raised up with Christ and I am born again. I repent of all my sins and I shall be baptized in the Name of the Lord and I shall receive the gift of the Holy Ghost according to Acts 2:38. I proclaim the precious blood of Jesus over my soul and I am saved. I will testify that Jesus is Lord of Lords and King of Kings forever in my life. Thank You Father for writing my name down in the Lamb's Book of Life. I am redeemed from the curse of the law and the sin of death. I now have eternal life because I believe.

Amen.

Appendix
The
Jerusalem Covenant
Document

As of this day, Jerusalem Day, the twenty-eighth day of the month of Iyar in the year five thousand seven hundred fifty-two; one thousand nine hundred and twenty-two years after the destruction of the Second Temple; forty-four years since the founding of the State of Israel; twenty-five years since the Six Day War during which the Israel Defense Forces, in defense of our very existence, broke through the walls of the city and restored the Temple Mount and the unity of Jerusalem; twelve years since the Knesset of Israel reestablished that Jerusalem, "unified and whole, is the Capital of Israel; the State of Israel is the State of the Jewish People" and the Capital of Israel is the Capital of the People in Israel. We have gathered together in Zion, national leaders and heads of our communities everywhere, to enter into a covenant with Jerusalem, as was done by the leaders of our nation and all the people of

Israel upon Israel's return to its Land from the Babylonian exile; and the people and their leaders vowed to 'dwell in Jerusalem, the Holy City.'

Once again, "our feet stand within your gates, O Jerusalem – Jerusalem built as a city joined together 'which' unites the people of Israel to one another", and links heavenly Jerusalem with earthly Jerusalem."

We have returned to the place that the Lord vowed to bestow upon the descendants of Abraham, Father of our Nation; to the City of David, King of Israel; where Solomon, son of David, built a Holy Temple; a Capital City which became the Mother of all Israel; a metropolis for justice and righteousness and for the wisdom and insights of the ancient world; where a Second Temple was erected in the days of Ezra and Nehemiah. In this city the prophets of the Lord prophesied; in this City the Sages taught Torah; in this City the Sanhedrin convened in session in its stone chamber. "For there were the seats of Justice, the Throne of the House of David", "for out of Zion shall go forth Torah, and the Word of the Lord from Jerusalem."

Today, as of old, we hold fast to the truth of the words of the Prophets of Israel, that all the inhabitants of the world shall enter within the gates of Jerusalem: "And it shall come to pass at the end of days, the mountain of the House of the Lord will be well established at the peak of the mountains and will tower above the hills, and all the nations shall stream towards it." Each and every nation will live in it by its own faith: "For all the nations will go forward, each with its own Divine Name; we shall go in the name of the Lord our God forever and ever." And in this spirit the Knesset of the State of Israel has enacted a law: the places holy to the peoples of all religions shall be protected from any desecration and from any restriction of free access to them.

Jerusalem – peace and tranquillity shall reign in the city: "Pray for the peace of Jerusalem; may those who love you be tranquil. May there be peace within your walls, and tranquillity within your palaces. Out of Jerusalem, a message of peace went forth and shall yet go forth again to all the inhabitants of the earth: "And they shall beat their swords into plowshares, and their spears into pruning-hooks; nation will not lift up sword against nation, nor shall they learn war any more. Our sages, peace be upon them, said: In the future, The Holy One, the Blessed, will comfort Jerusalem only with peace.

From this place, we once again take this vow: "If I forget thee, O Jerusalem, may my right hand lose its strength; may my tongue cleave to my palate if I do not remember you, if I do not raise up Jerusalem at the very height of my rejoicing."

And with all these understandings, we enter into this Covenant and write: We shall bind you to us forever; we shall bind you to us with faithfulness, with righteousness and justice, with steadfast love and compassion. We love you, O Jerusalem, with eternal love, with unbounded love, under siege and when liberated from the yoke of oppressors. We have been martyred for you; we have yearned for you, we have clung to you. Our faithfulness to you we shall bequeath to our children after us. Forevermore, our home shall be within you.

Book/Tape Order List

"A Miracle In The Making" The story of Evangelist Richard Madison's healing and conversion to the Lord, is living proof of God's promises, resurrection and power. From death to a full-time teaching and healing ministry, Richard is truly one of God's chosen people. Let Richard show you how you can have miracles in your life. In God's eyes, nothing in your life is impossible.

Miracle In The Making - $10.00
Cassette Tape Only - $3.00
Video Tape Only - $18.00
All Three Items - $28.00
        Add $2.00 shipping and handling

Signs Of Jesus' Return - Will The Millennial Reign Begin By 2003 - 2 tape cassette set in vinal holder - $8.00
2 Hour Video - $20.00

Write for other prophetic update material.

Richard L. Madison
Rt. 2, Box 207
Oakman, AL 35579

Name_____

Address_____ _____

City_____State_____Zip_____